· THE · BLUE RIDER

THE YELLOW COW SEES THE WORLD IN BLUE

Prestel
Munich · New York

There was once a young Russian artist who went to Munich to learn to paint. There he met a woman, also an artist, and fell in love ...

This is how the story of the Blue Rider began. It is the story of a handful of young artists who came together and painted very different pictures from those by earlier artists — pictures that confused people because there were yellow cows, green people, red trees, or blue horses in them, or just as bright spots of color. Other artists also had different ideas about how cows and people, trees and horses should be represented.

Wassily Kandinsky — this was the name of the young Russian artist — went to Munich from Moscow at the beginning of this century. There he met Gabriele Münter, who had come to study painting with him, and fell in love with her. Soon Kandinsky became the leader of a group of painter-friends who had similar ideas about art. They spent a lot of time together as friends do, and attempted to organize exhibitions of their pictures. Kandinsky and Münter first became friends with the Russian artist couple Alexej Jawlensky and Marianne von Werefkin, who like Kandinsky had gone to Munich to study painting. Franz Marc and August Macke joined the group, and later Paul Klee. Kandinsky and his friends chose Saint George as their patron saint and called the group the "Blue Rider," because they liked both horses and the color blue. Their new art would take the world by storm.

1

For many years, they worked together and painted their brilliant pictures, which are admired throughout the world today. You can see many of the best ones at a gallery called the Lenbachhaus in Munich.

Franz Marc
Blue Horse I   1911

There is a lot to see here: a castle on a hill, a large church with a cemetery at the right, a little chapel hidden at the left, a rowboat on the river.

2 And many people: mothers with children, lovers, wise old men, a traveler with a long beard.

A blue knight bursts through the picture, and his sword, even his hair, are blue.

Kandinsky's figures in their fantastic garments resemble figures from Russian fairy tales. With its many dots, the picture resembles an exquisite, brightly patterned carpet. It seems exotic and unreal — like a story-book dream in living color.

3

Wassily Kandinsky
Motley Life   1907

A sweep of colors in blue, red, yellow, and green — is this really by the same artist?

If we look closely, we can see the same castle on a hill, a rider in red robes on a white horse. And isn't that a pair of lovers again at the right?

Kandinsky and his friends did not just want to paint mountains, towns, riders, and lovers as they saw them; they wanted to express something else in their paintings. Colors were feelings, dreams, thoughts, memories. So blue symbolizes a yearning for heaven, yellow shows the joy of light and warmth, red stands for strength and the force of life.

Music was very important for Kandinsky who said that everything in the world "rings." Colors make his pictures sing, just as notes make up music.

Wassily Kandinsky
Mountain 1909

Three riders hurl
themselves *down*
the hill at a wild gallop as if they are being chased.
Trees, mountains, rocks, light, air, and sky flow around
them in colorful dots and dashes.

6   The RED setting sun shines above them.

Kandinsky was a magician conjuring tricks with images and paint.
All of his horses and landscapes look completely different from those in this painting
by Wilhelm von Kobell, who had lived about a hundred years before him. In earlier
paintings, horses were black, white, gray, or brown, and you could tell from the
position of their legs if they were galloping or not.

Kandinsky
also created
light and
movement
by means
of colors
and shapes

Wilhelm von Kobell
After the Hunt at Lake Constance 1833

Wassily Kandinsky
Romantic Landscape   1911

Wassily Kandinsky

Improvisation 21a   1911

8

Kandinsky's paintings are often puzzles. If we compare the picture on the left with the small painting on glass (below) that he had painted just before, we suddenly recognize the castle on the hill, the lovers, and the three riders racing through the landscape. Two ghostlike figures appear in the right foreground, and behind them we can see a rowboat on the water.

Wassily Kandinsky

With Sun   1911

It is not really possible to recognize objects in these pictures. But using our imagination, the colors and shapes take on new forms, and the pictures tell little stories.

If we look carefully, we can see the rowboat here. The long black strokes are the oars, and above the red semicircle of the boat are the black shapes of the rowers. The expanding red spot at the right is all that is left of a rider.

One spring day in 1908, Wassily Kandinsky and Gabriele Münter discovered the delightful village of Murnau at the foot of the Alps. They described the place enthusiastically to Alexej Jawlensky and Marianne von Werefkin. From that time on, they went frequently to Murnau together to paint the village and the beautiful Bavarian landscape.

In Murnau

Wassily Kandinky and Gabriele Münter on an excursion

At first, we see only bright spots of color in the picture opposite. But when we let our eyes wander through it, it becomes a landscape. Can you find the church? (We saw a different one in the first picture.) And — right at the front, but very well hidden — is it the rider?

Gabriele Münter bought a house in Murnau. Her neighbors called it the "Russians' House" because so many of her painter-friends were Russians. Münter also painted the house later.

Gabriele Münter
The Russians' House 1931

Wassily Kandinsky
Murnau with Church I 1910

10

12   This picture of two people relaxing in an alpine meadow is made up of spots of color outlined in black. The clear, bright colors breathe with the joy of living and the artists' love of the Bavarian landscape.

Kandinsky and Münter collected paintings on glass, woodcuts, and other objects of folk art. Their house in Murnau and their apartment in Munich were full of these things, which appear over and over again in their pictures. On the wall in this picture, which shows Kandinsky and Erma Bossi — another artist — sitting together at a table, we can make out a painted plate next to colorful pictures, vessels, and figures on a shelf.

Kandinsky is wearing traditional Bavarian dress with short pants.

Kandinsky in the garden

Gabriele Münter
Kandinsky and Erma Bossi, after Dinner 1912

Gabriele Münter
Jawlensky and Werefkin 1908/09

A red road crosses a landscape glowing with color, its forms angular and distorted. Turquoise mountains appear behind variegated trees with lilac shadows. Clearly, it is summer.

This picture makes us think of the warm ground

under our bare feet.

Jawlensky was not interested in painting the landscape

exactly as he saw it. He wanted to capture it

as he had experienced it for a single moment.

Colors and shape are light and warmth

and air and feeling.

t was in Murnau that the artists discovered the true beauty of the countryside. For several years, it remained an important theme in their paintings.

Alexej Jawlensky
Murnau Landscape   1909

You are being watched

Alexej Jawlensky
*Portrait of the Dancer
Alexander Sacharoff* 1909

Above a bright red dress, black eyes stare out at us from a
white face. A mysterious smile plays over the red lips.

Is this a man or a woman?

Alexej Jawlensky
Maturity c. 1912

16

The portrait of Alexander Sacharoff came into
being one night when the dancer visited Jawlensky
in his studio in make-up and costume before going
to the theater. It was Sacharoff's eyes, his gaze, that
fascinated the painter.

When Jawlensky painted people, he was not
interested in the particular shape of a nose or wart
on someone's chin, but in the expression on their
face. He wanted to paint people's feelings, not their
appearances.

Much later, he assembled faces that radiate calm
from a few lines and rectangles.

Alexej Jawlensky
*Meditation on
Gold Ground* 1936

Green eyes, yellow skin, blue-green hair —
who can this be? Strong black lines outline
the nose, mouth, and eyes.
And once again, she is watching you.

Franz and Maria Marc
and their dog Russi

Window into Animals' Souls

Franz Marc was especially close to Kandinsky. Together they invented the name "Blue Rider" and wrote a book, the *Blaue Reiter Almanac*, in which they explained their ideas about art. Marc lived with his wife Maria in Sindelsdorf, near Murnau, and they visited Kandinsky frequently.

18   Here we glimpse a crouching tiger. All of the shapes are angular. We sense the animal's strength and energy, and know it is ready to

pounce !

Franz Marc
Cows, Yellow-Red-Green 1912

The bellowing yellow of the cow expresses happiness. "The yellow cow sees the world in blue," wrote the poet Theodor Däubler about this picture.

Franz Marc
The Tiger 1912

Franz Marc did not reproduce reality in his paintings either. Colors and shapes served

as an expression of something quite different. Marc dreamed of a better world.

He wanted to see the world through the spirits of animals: "Can we imagine how

animals see us and nature? Surely there can't be a more intriguing thought for an artist

than to show nature through the eyes of an animal? How does a horse, or an eagle,

a deer or a dog see the world?"

20

It is night, the dark sky presses its blue into the picture.
A deer is curled up in a hollow. It finds safety in a mysterious
fairy-tale forest filled with color.

Franz Marc almost always painted

animals. He loved them more than

people and was fascinated by their

innocence: animals never pretend;

they are always honest.

Franz Marc
Deer in a Monastery Garden   1912

This picture appears to be seen
through a kaleidoscope. The nervous fluttering of
the bird breaks into splinters of different colors.
Only if we look a second time can we see
two other birds.

22

Franz Marc
Red and Blue Horse   1912

STILLNESS and MOTION
are also present in the
picture of two horses side
by side. One of them
jumps around friskily,
the other stands quietly
and looks thoughtfully
at the ground.

RED is lively,

BLUE is quiet.

Ideal Worlds

Stroll among trees and bushes alive with parrots and cockatoos,
lean over the railings, watch flamingos, and pet the deer —
the zoo is shown as an ideal world.

24 Although several years younger than Franc Marc, August Macke became a very good friend and
met the other artists through him. Macke loved to watch people out for a Sunday stroll, observe

others sitting in cafés
or window-shopping,
like this elegant lady
who examines the
display in a hat shop.
Macke's ideal world is
full of sun and peole
enjoying themselves.

August Macke
Milliner's Shop 1913

Franz Marc
Two Blue Horses in front of a red rock,
Postcard to Kandinsky,
21 May 1913

When not everyone had a telephone, people would write to one another more frequently than they do today. We still have many postcards that were made by Franz Marc, who decorated them with his own pictures. These enchanting greeting cards were so beautiful that everyone who received them kept them carefully. Often, they contained such routine messages as:

"[Dear Kandinsky] ... Both of you should come with Sacharoff ... and the 4 of us can have a pleasant supper together ..."

Franz Marc,
Four Foxes, Postcard to Kandinsky,
4 February 1913

Franz Marc
Landscape with Red Animal,
Postcard to Alfred Kubin,
18 March 1913

"Dear Kandinsky, ... We are coming to town on Sunday evening. May we report to your place for the evening? At about 7:30. Then we can have a good chat again. Hopefully, this is convenient. With best wishes from us to you, your Fz. Marc."

"Dear Kandinsky, Your book is simply wonderful ... I'm absolutely enchanted ..."

"Dear K., I'm ill, strained the muscles in my back, so simply cannot come..."

Franz Marc
Red and Blue Horse,
Postcard to Kandinsky,
5 April 1913

Franz Marc
Vermilion Greeting,
Postcard to Kandinsky,
9 April 1913

Franz Marc was a close friend of the poet Else Lasker-Schüler, who lived in Berlin. In her poem-letters she called him *"My dear, dear, dear, dear blue rider Franz Marc"* or *"Ruben, my half-brother,"* and signed herself *"Jussuf Abigail of Thebes," "The little toy king Jussuf,"* or *"Your poor toy prince."*

"The Blue Rider presents your highness with its blue horse" appeared on one of his cards, and she answered: *"The blue rider is there — a lovely sentence, five words — pure stars. Now I feel like the moon. Live in the clouds ..."*

Franz Marc
Two Animals,
Postcard to
Kandinsky,
15 February 1913

27

In 1914, Macke went to Tunisia with two friends, the painters Paul Klee and Louis Moilliet. En route he recorded everything he saw in watercolors and drawings, and when he returned home, he painted his most brilliant pictures.

Left: Paul Klee

Right: August Macke (on the donkey) and Paul Klee in Tunisia

A Trip to Africa

August Macke
St. Germain near Tunis 1914

The green of the Arab with a red fez shines out against the vibrant blue wall of the café, whose door and floor are orange. In the foreground, a shrill yellow chair, above that lush green leaves — the African sun made Macke's colors even stronger, as if they were on fire.

August Macke
Turkish Café 1914

The End

In 1914, when the First World War broke out, everything ended abruptly. All Russians, including Kandinsky, Jawlensky, and Werefkin, had to leave Germany. Other artists served as soldiers in the war. Macke and Marc died at the ages of twenty-seven and thirty-six on the battlefield in France.
The beautiful dream of color and shapes was over.

30   This picture by Paul Klee shows the ghastly, lifeless emptiness left by the war.

Paul Klee
Destroyed Place   1920

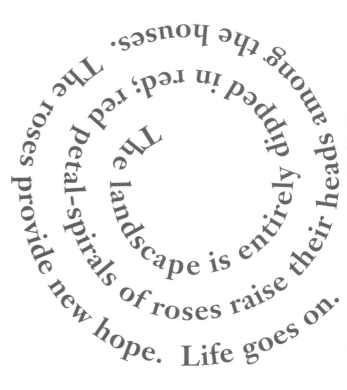

The roses provide new hope. Life goes on. The landscape is entirely dipped in red; red petal-spirals of roses raise their heads among the houses.

Paul Klee
Rose Garden   1920

The story of the Blue Rider in Munich ends here

Those who survived the war scattered in all directions. Paul Klee was the last to leave Munich, and went to teach at the Bauhaus, a newly established art school, in Weimar. There he met Wassily Kandinsky again, who had been in Moscow. Alexej Jawlensky also arrived in Weimar. Together with the painter Lyonel Feininger, Kandinsky, Jawlensky, and Klee established a new artists' group at the Bauhaus, called the Blue Four ... but that is another story.

What remains in Munich are some of the most beautiful pictures of all time. They are carefully preserved at the Lenbachhaus — a gallery in which the colorful pictures of the Blue Rider hang on BLUE, GREEN, RED, or YELLOW walls.

33

List of Illustrations

All paintings illustrated are at the Städtische Galerie im Lenbachhaus, Munich

(Photographs by Simone Gänsheimer, Ernst Jank, and Jörg Koopmann)

Alexej Jawlensky

Murnau Landscape, 1909
oil on cardboard, 19 $^7/_8$ x 21 $^1/_2$ in.
(50.5 x 54.5 cm)

Portrait of the Dancer Alexander Sacharoff, 1909
oil on cardboard, 27 $^3/_8$ x 26 $^1/_8$ in.
(69.5 x 66.5 cm)

Maturity, c. 1912
oil on cardboard, 21 x 19 $^1/_2$ in.
(53.5 x 49.5 cm)

Meditation on Gold Ground, 1936
oil on cardboard, 5 $^1/_2$ x 4 $^3/_8$ in.
(14 x 11 cm)

Wassily Kandinsky

Motley Life, 1907
tempera on canvas, 51 $^1/_4$ x 63 in.
(130 x 162.5 cm)

Mountain, 1909
oil on canvas, 42 $^7/_8$ x 42 $^7/_8$ in.
(109 x 109 cm)

Murnau with Church I, 1910
oil on cardboard, 25 $^1/_2$ x 19 $^3/_4$ in.
(64.7 x 50.2 cm)

Romantic Landscape, 1911
oil on canvas, 37 $^1/_4$ x 50 $^3/_4$ in.
(94.3 x 129 cm)

With Sun, 1911
Painting on glass, 12 x 15 $^7/_8$ in.
(30.6 x 40.3 cm)

Improvisation 21a, 1911
oil on canvas, 37 $^3/_4$ x 41 $^3/_8$ in.
(96 x 105 cm)

Improvisation 26 – Rowing, 1912
oil on canvas, 38 $^1/_4$ x 42 $^3/_8$ in.
(97 x 107.5 cm)

Paul Klee

Destroyed Place, 1920
oil on paper mounted on gray-blue cardboard on plain cardboard, with a narrow strip of tarnished silver around the image, 8 $^3/_4$ x 7 $^5/_8$ in.
(22.3 x 19.5 cm)

Rose Garden, 1920
oil on cardboard, 19 $^1/_4$ x 16 $^3/_4$ in.
(49 x 42.5 cm)

August Macke

Zoological Garden I, 1912
oil on canvas, 23 x 38 $^5/_8$ in.
(58.5 x 98 cm)

Milliner's Shop, 1913
oil on canvas, 21 $^1/_2$ x 17 $^3/_8$ in.
(54.5 x 44 cm)

Turkish Café, 1914
oil on board, 23 $^5/_8$ x 13 $^3/_4$ in.
(60 x 35 cm)

St. Germain near Tunis, 1914
watercolor on paper, 10 $^1/_4$ x 8 $^1/_4$ in.
(26 x 21 cm)

Franz Marc

Blue Horse I, 1911
oil on canvas, 44 x 33 $^1/_4$ in.
(112 x 84.5 cm)

The Tiger, 1912
oil on canvas, 43 $^3/_4$ x 43 $^7/_8$ in.
(111 x 111.5 cm)

Cows, Yellow-Red-Green, 1912
oil on canvas, 24 $^3/_8$ x 34 $^1/_2$ in.
(62 x 87.5 cm)

Deer in the Forest II, 1912
oil on canvas, 43 $^1/_4$ x 31 $^7/_8$ in.
(110 x 81 cm)

Deer in a Monastery Garden, 1912
oil on canvas, 29 $^3/_4$ x 39 $^3/_4$ in.
(75.7 x 101 cm)

Red and Blue Horse, 1912
tempera on paper, 10 $^3/_8$ x 13 $^1/_2$ in.
(26.3 x 34.3 cm)

Four Foxes,
Postcard to Kandinsky, 4 February 1913
watercolor on paper, 5 $^1/_2$ x 3 $^1/_2$ in.
(14 x 9 cm)

Two Animals,
Postcard to Kandinsky, 15 February 1913
watercolor on paper, 5 $^1/_2$ x 3 $^1/_2$ in.
(14 x 9 cm)

Landscape with Red Animal,
Postcard to Alfred Kubin, 18 March 1913
tempera on paper, 3 $^1/_2$ x 5 $^1/_2$ in.
(9 x 14 cm)

Red and Blue Horse,
Postcard to Kandinsky, 5 April 1913
watercolor on paper, 3 $^1/_2$ x 5 $^1/_2$ in.
(9 x 14 cm)

Vermilion Greetings,
Postcard to Kandinsky, 9 April 1913
tempera on paper, 5 $^1/_2$ x 3 $^1/_2$ in.
(14 x 9 cm)

Two Blue Horses in front of a Red Rock,
Postcard to Kandinsky, 21 May 1913
tempera on paper, varnished,
5 $^1/_2$ x 3 $^1/_2$ in. (14 x 9 cm)

The Birds, 1914
oil on canvas, 42 $^7/_8$ x 39 $^3/_8$ in.
(109 x 100 cm)

Gabriele Münter

Jawlensky and Werefkin, 1908/09
oil on cardboard, 12 $^7/_8$ x 17 $^1/_2$ in.
(32.7 x 44.5 cm)

Kandinsky and Erma Bossi, after Dinner, 1912
oil on canvas, 37 $^5/_8$ x 49 $^3/_8$ in.
(95.5 x 125.5 cm)

The Russians' House, 1931
oil on canvas, 16 $^3/_4$ x 22 $^1/_2$ in.
(42.5 x 57 cm)